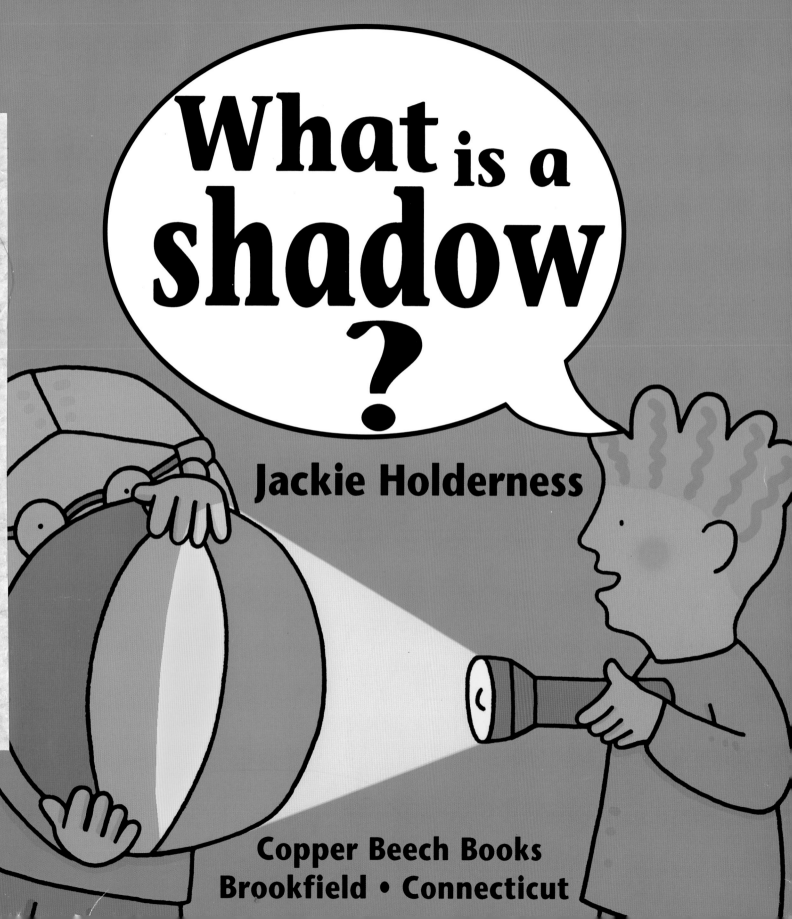

How? What? Why?

What is a shadow?

Jackie Holderness

Copper Beech Books
Brookfield • Connecticut

Why does it get dark at night?

Amy, Steve, Jo, and Zack are going to the fair with Amy's mom and dad. It has been a sunny day, but Amy sees that the sun is starting to go down. "Don't look straight at the sun," says Amy's mom. "It can hurt your eyes."

In the day we get light from the sun. At night there's no sun, so it's dark.

Why does it get dark at night?

2

3

Let's see how the children find out.

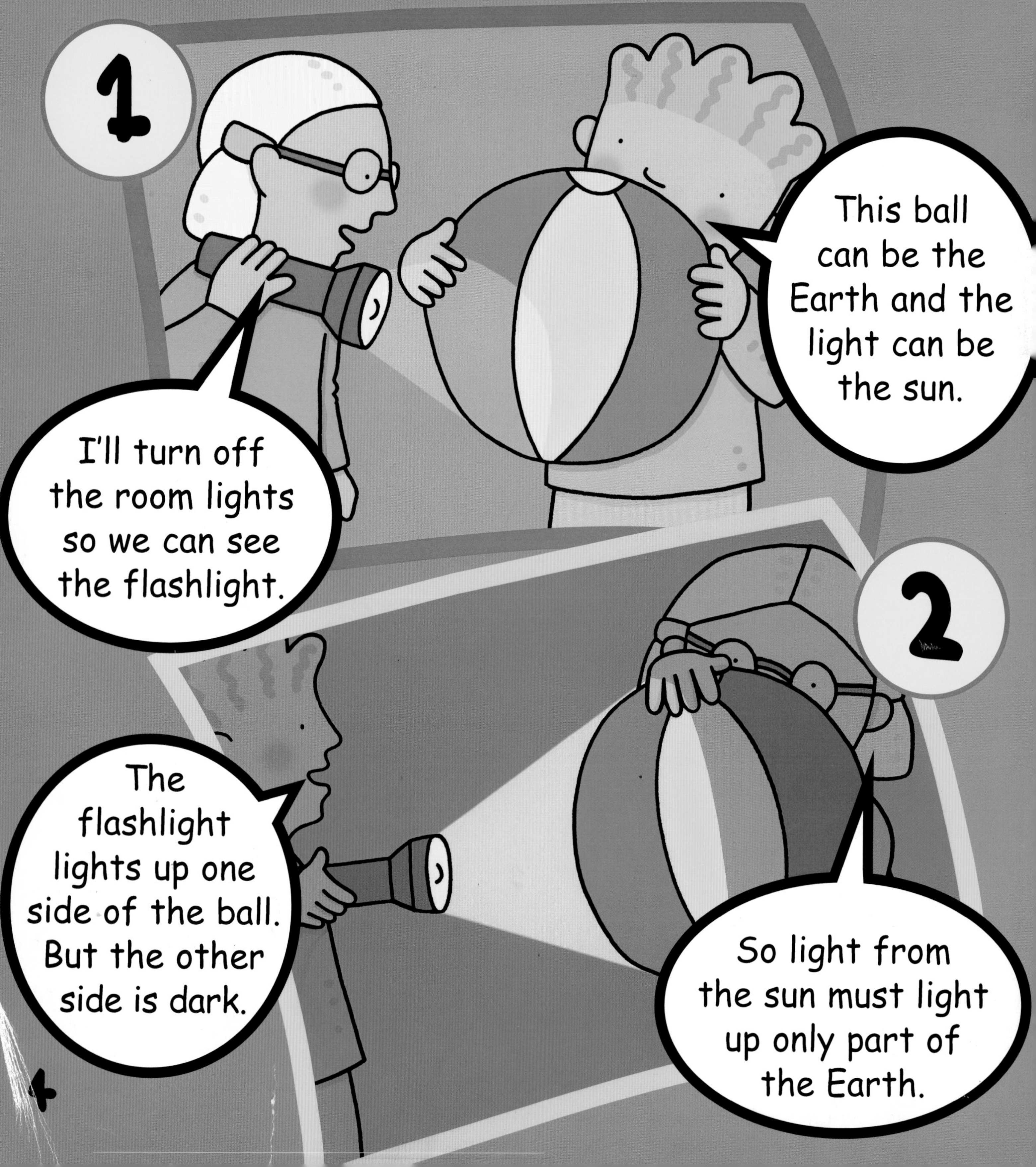

3

Let's say we live where that mark is. During the day we are in the sun's light.

4

At night the sun must move or the Earth must spin so we are in the dark.

Why it works

Light from the sun lights up the Earth. It only lights up one side, so the other side of the Earth is dark. The sun may look as if it's moving across the sky, but it's the Earth that moves. It spins around once every 24 hours, so we spend some time in the light (day) and some time in the dark (night).

Solve the puzzle!

How many light sources are there in your home? A light source is anything that gives off light, like a flashlight or a lamp. Write down a list, then see how you can make this into a chart on page 22.

What is a shadow?

The sun gets lower and lower in the sky. The children's shadows get longer and longer. "Look at our shadows," says Amy's mom. "They're a bit spooky!"

What is a shadow?

I think a shadow is the shape made when something gets in the way of the light.

6

7

Let's see how the children find out.

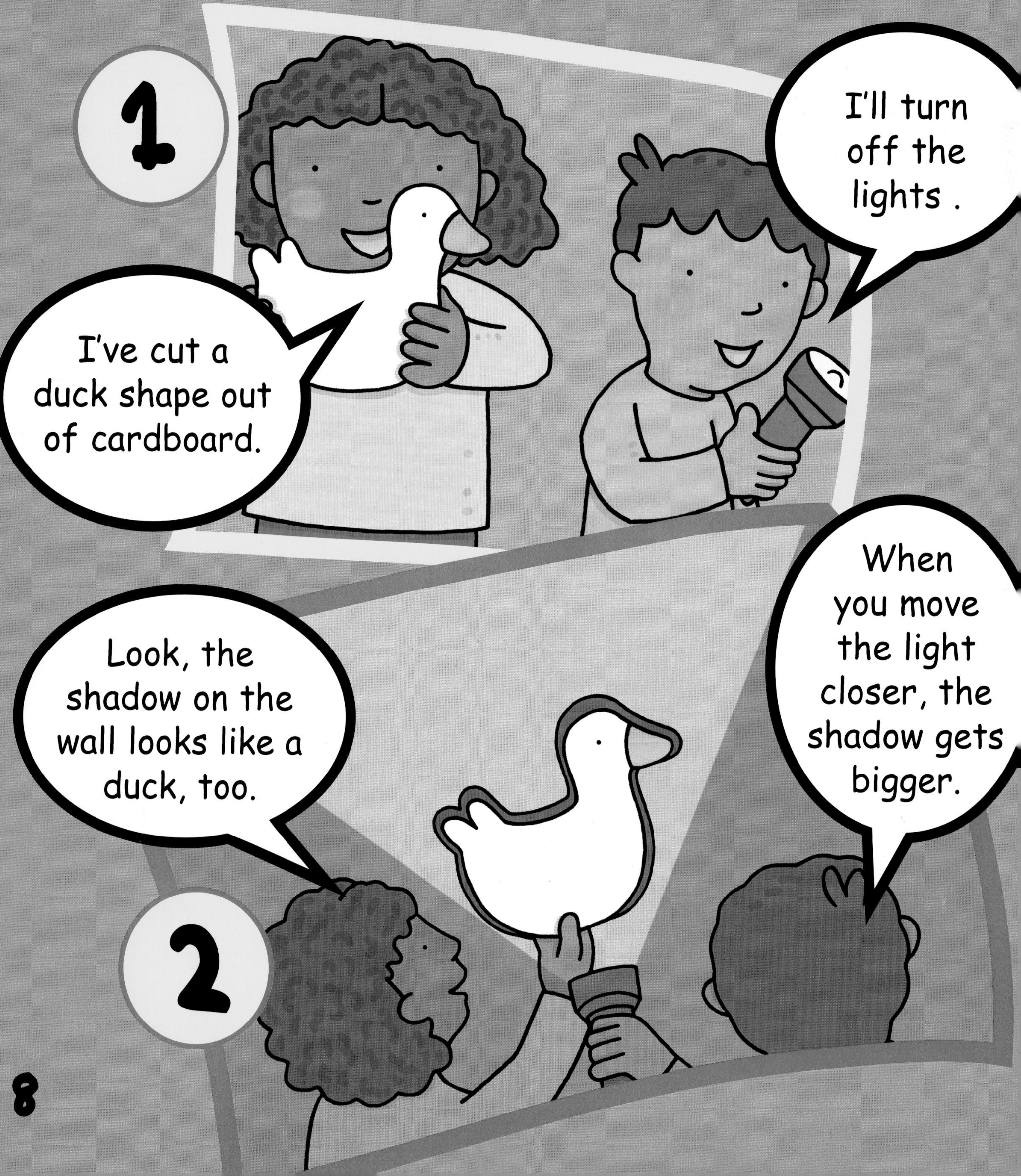

Why it works

Shadows are places where the light from the sun or a lamp cannot reach. They are made when light cannot pass through something. A shadow appears opposite the light source, but its shape depends on where the light source is. On a sunny day, stand a stick in the ground and watch its shadow move and change shape. When the sun gets low in the sky, the stick's shadow will get longer.

Solve the puzzle

Does everything have a shadow? Try shining a flashlight through a glass or a pair of sunglasses.

How can you be seen at night?

The sun goes down and it is soon dark. Suddenly, a jogger in dark clothes runs past the children and nearly bumps into them. Steve does not see her and jumps with surprise.

I didn't see that woman running!

Look out! Here comes someone else on a bicycle!

I think the cyclist's bright clothes help us to see him.
Maybe his shiny belt reflects the street lights.
What do you think?

Let's see how the children find out.

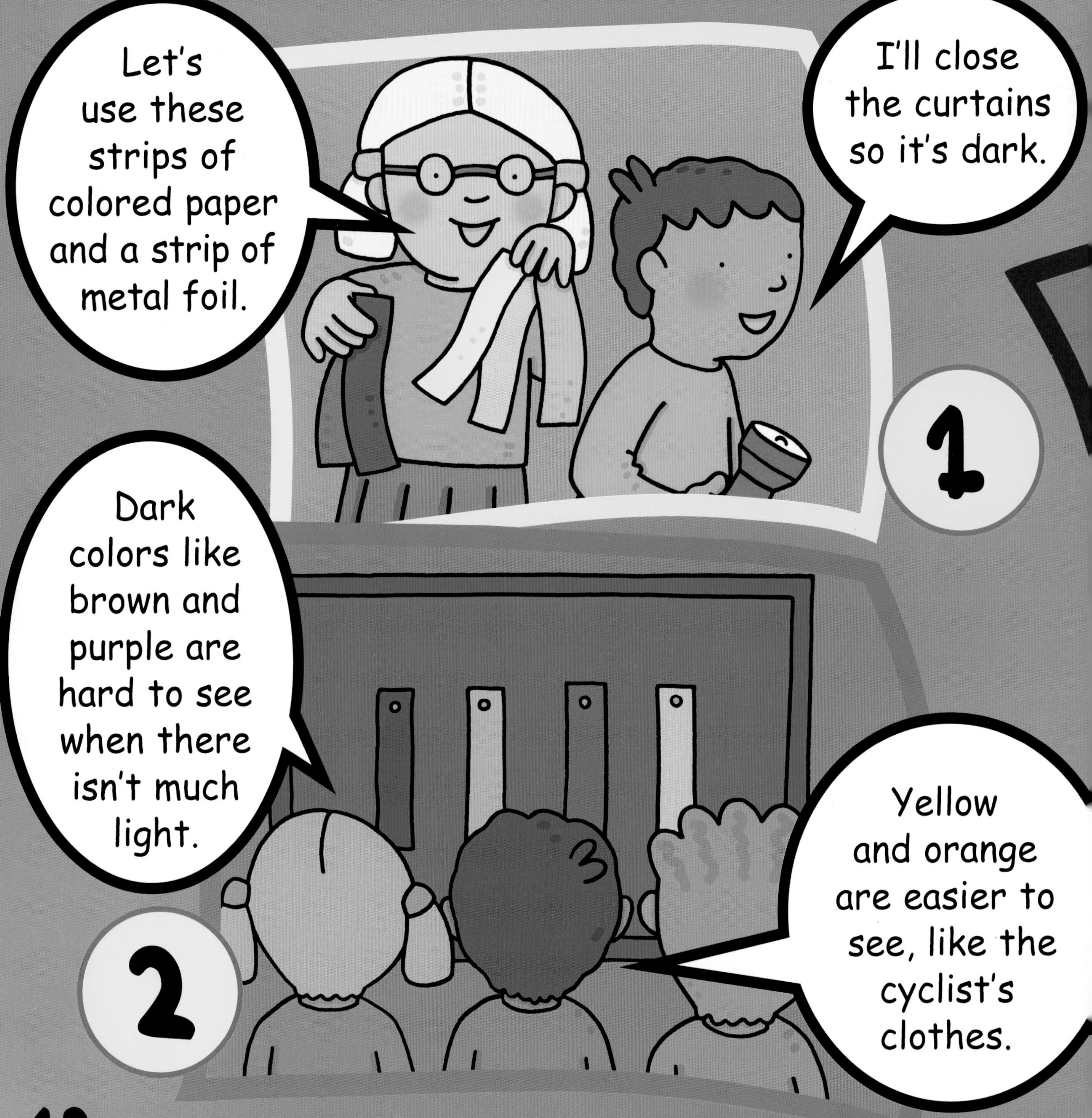

When you shine a light on the metal foil it glitters.

The light must bounce off it. That's why it was easy to see the shiny belt under the street lights.

3

Why it works

We see things because light from the sun or a lamp bounces off them into our eyes. We say the light reflects off them. Pale colors reflect more light than dark colors. So at night, people who wear white or yellow are more likely to be seen than people in dark clothes. Shiny objects reflect a lot of light. We see them when some of this reflected light enters our eyes.

Solve the puzzle

What is moonlight? Do you think the moon gives off light like the sun?

Why are lights brighter close up?

As the children walk toward the fair, they can see the big wheel. When they get close, they see it is covered with lots of bright colored lights.

The lights on the wheel are very bright.

It must be because there are so many of them.

Let's see how the children find out.

When the light is farther away, the circle is much bigger.

The light must spread out as the flashlight gets farther away. It's dimmer, too.

That's why the lights at the fair were dim far away but bright close up.

Why it works

The closer you are to a light, the brighter it seems. Think about how headlights get brighter the closer a car is to you. That's because light spreads out as it gets farther away from a light source such as a lamp. So the flashlight makes a small, bright circle of light when it's near the wall. When it's farther away, the circle is larger but dimmer.

Solve the puzzle

Why are fireworks set off at night? Think about how bright a flashlight is when you shine it in the dark and how bright when you turn on the room lights.

How do mirrors work

The children visit the hall of mirrors. In one corner there are three mirrors facing each other. When Jo looks in them, she can see lots of reflections.

Wow, there are lots of me! How does it work?

Maybe the light bounces from one mirror to the other one and back again.

I agree. Light must bounce off a mirror just as it bounces off shiny metal foil.
I wonder if a mirror can make the light change direction.
What do you think?

Let's see how the children find out.

3

When I move the mirror, I can make the light change direction.

You can even bounce the light back off this mirror! So that's why you saw lots of reflections.

Why it works

Light travels in straight lines called rays. When light hits a mirror, it bounces off, or is reflected, in a new direction. If you look straight at a mirror, the light bouncing off your body hits the mirror then bounces straight back, so you see yourself. With more than one mirror, light bounces from one mirror to another. This makes lots of reflections.

Solve the puzzle!

Why did one mirror make Steve look strange? Find a big shiny spoon and see what you look like in it!

Did you solve the puzzles?

How many light sources are in your home?

Light sources can light up a whole room or just a small area. You can make a chart of them:

Light up whole room	Light up small area
Room lights	Flashlights
Candles	Spotlights
Strip lights	Bedside lamp

Did you find any other lights? Lights on machines tell us if they are turned on. These lights are often red or green.

Can light pass through any solid objects?

Yes. Light can pass through clear materials like glass. If you shine a flashlight at a glass, you can see the light on the other side. Some materials only let some light through, like the dark glass in a pair of sunglasses (Jo wears a pair on page 3). Sunglasses protect your eyes when the sun's light is too bright for them.

What is moonlight?

The moon is not a light source. It just reflects light from the sun. However, stars make their own light. They are like our sun, but are very far away.

Why are fireworks set off at night?

Fireworks are set off at night because during the day the bright light of the sun would make them hard to see. Room lights also make a flashlight hard to see, so try experiments with a flashlight in a dark room!

Why did one mirror make Steve look strange?

When light hits a curved shiny surface, such as a curved mirror or a metal spoon, it is reflected in many different directions. This can make your face look squashed or stretched. Does your face look the same on both sides of a spoon?

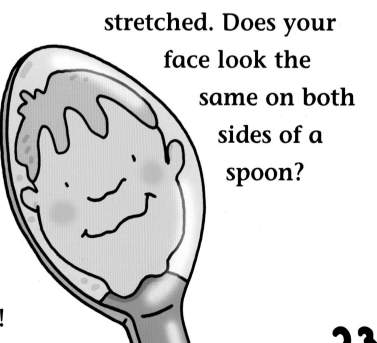

23

Index

© Aladdin Books Ltd 2002

10 9 8 7 6 5 4 3 2 1

Designed and produced by
Aladdin Books Ltd
28 Percy Street
London W1T 2BZ

First published in
the United States in 2002 by
Copper Beech Books,
an imprint of
The Millbrook Press
2 Old New Milford Road
Brookfield, Connecticut 06804

ISBN 0-7613-2821-1 (Library bdg.)
ISBN 0-7613-1739-2 (Trade h'cover)
ISBN 0-7613-1840-2 (Paper ed.)

Cataloging-in-Publication data
is on file at the Library of Congress.

Printed in U.A.E.
All rights reserved

Editor
Jim Pipe

Science Consultants
Helen Wilson and David Coates
Westminster Institute of Education
Oxford Brookes University, England

Science Tester
Alex Laar

Design
Flick, Book Design and Graphics

Illustration
Jo Moore